Original title:
Is Life's Meaning the Same as a Good Nap?

Author: Wyatt Kensington
ISBN HARDBACK: 978-1-80566-077-4
ISBN PAPERBACK: 978-1-80566-372-0

Twilight Thoughts

In twilight's glow, we ponder deep,
Should we count our dreams or simply sleep?
A pillow's hug, a blanket's fold,
Provides a wisdom not often told.

In snores, we find the rumbling truth,
That naps may hold the secrets of youth.
With droopy eyes and cozy sighs,
We battle daily life's silly lies.

In Search of Peaceful Slumber

With a quest for dreams, I roam the night,
Chasing cozy clouds, oh what a sight!
The couch, the chair, my comfy bed,
Each one calls me with whispers said.

In snoozy lands, my troubles fade,
Life's complex puzzles seem less unmade.
A dreamt-up feast, or flying cat,
All thanks to a catnap or two; imagine that!

The Restful Quest

A journey begins with a gentle yawn,
To far-off fields, I am drawn!
The roadmap's paved with slumber sweet,
Who knew rest could be such a treat?

With every snore, adventures unfold,
Lazily, I travel, my dreams untold.
Yet mornings strike, I wake with a gasp,
Was that a dragon? Just a nap's clasp!

Midnight Musings

When midnight strikes, I ponder fate,
Should I work or just hibernate?
With heavy lids and a sleepy grin,
The land of dreams calls me back again.

I muse in verses, half-asleep,
Life's joys are rich, yet naps run deep.
So here's my thought, as I start to sway,
Let's nap our worries slowly away!

The Stillness Between Moments

In the cozy hug of sheets,
The world drifts lightly away.
Counting sheep on soft retreat,
Time's a game we love to play.

Beneath the ticking clock's hum,
Dreams parade in funny hats.
Life pauses, whispers, 'Here I come!'
But first, take that well-earned nap!

A Brief Caress of Time

With a wink, the pillow calls,
Saying, 'Come and rest a while.'
Grass grows, and on us it falls,
As slumber wraps us in a smile.

The clock may tangle hair and time,
But underneath this ruffled bed,
We schedule naps without a crime,
Where logic flies, and dreams are fed.

The Equilibrium of Rest

Balancing work like a tightrope,
A nap's a trampoline so grand.
Juggling tasks, losing hope,
Yet waking up feels like a brand.

In that quiet of the midday,
There's laughter in the sleepy blight.
A nap's a dance, a silly sway,
Where consciousness takes a light flight.

Sandman's Wisdom

The Sandman came with frosty wings,
Whispering secrets of the snooze.
He knows the joy that dreaming brings,
Laughing at the morning blues.

With each yawn, we drop our cares,
Floating on the clouds of warm.
Life's a joke, it lightly dares,
To play with dreams and keep us calm.

Time Stretched Over Fluff

On pillows soft, we drift away,
Chasing dreams that laugh and play.
The clock ticks slow, the world is hushed,
In snooze time's realm, our worries crushed.

The cat thinks it's a race to snore,
While I discover a secret door.
Into the realm of sighs and hums,
Where every good nap happily comes.

Daydreams and Deep Slumbers

In sunlight's glow, a cozy bed,
I ponder life and toast my bread.
The world outside can wait awhile,
As dreams bring forth a napping smile.

Fluffy clouds, my sleepy friends,
Whispering tales that never end.
In slumber's verse, I dance and sway,
While my alarm clock cries 'Not today!'

Answers in the Quiet Hour

In silence deep, the thoughts take flight,
Philosophy found in the night.
Yet all that's gained from pondering,
Is how to sleep through anything.

With snuggled heart and fluffy plight,
I search for truths in cozy light.
A yawn is wisdom's only friend,
As nap time dreams begin to blend.

The Poetry Beneath Closed Eyes

Alive to dreams that softly sing,
In slumber, I'm a wandering king.
With every nap, a world appears,
Where laughter flows and joy endears.

Yet as I swoon through pillow skies,
Philosophy's a sleepy guise.
In blissful rest, the questions fade,
And all that's left is soft brigade.

Moments between Heartbeats

Lying down, my thoughts do race,
The pillow's soft, a warm embrace.
Chasing dreams that swiftly flee,
In these moments, I'm just me.

Time unravels, tick and tock,
The world outside is like a clock.
I drift away, no need to strive,
In slumber's grip, I feel alive.

Elysium Found in Dream

In the land of snores and sighs,
I soar high where the laughter lies.
Cupcakes rain from skies of blue,
All my worries bid adieu.

A cat's ballet, a dog's sweet song,
In this realm, nothing feels wrong.
With each wink, new joys collide,
In dreamland, I take my ride.

A Day's End Delight

The sun dips low, my eyelids droop,
In the corner, the nap gods stoop.
With a yawn, I claim my throne,
Peace and quiet, my favorite zone.

Beneath the blankets, I shall dwell,
In this cozy, cushy shell.
The world waits, but I won't fret,
For in this nap, I'm truly set.

Composing with Closed Eyes

With each breath, I find my flow,
On this soft cloud, I gently go.
Scribbling dreams, a funny tune,
In my mind, there's a bright full moon.

Ideas bounce, like kids at play,
In the land where dozers stay.
Notes and giggles fill the air,
Nap-time wisdom, oh so rare!

The Ethereal Nature of Rest

Amidst the chaos, I find my bliss,
A cozy blanket, a gentle kiss.
With pillows piled and dreams in tow,
I drift away, while time moves slow.

The world may spin, but I'm not there,
Just me and dreams, a perfect pair.
The clock strikes one, I snuggle tight,
My nap's the best part of the night.

Surrendering to Sweetness

Oh, sweet surrender, let me lay,
To close my eyes and drift away.
The dishes wait, the laundry too,
But first, a nap; I must pursue.

Dreams of cookies and endless fun,
In cozy realms, I'm number one.
As I recline, the stresses fade,
In nap-time heaven, I've got it made.

Flickers in the Half-Light

Sunbeams dancing on my face,
I find my bliss in this warm place.
Close my eyes and let thoughts flow,
In this daze, I dance with slow.

A cat nearby, he's snoozing deep,
We share a bond in blissful sleep.
A world of dreams, absurd and bright,
Where everything's whimsical, just right.

The Elixir of Repose

Life's a circus, full of cheer,
But napping's magic is what I revere.
With each snooze, I gain a treasure,
A little dose of pure pleasure.

So raise a pillow, toast a dream,
In this cozy nook, I reign supreme.
The world can wait, let troubles drop,
For in my slumber, I'm on top.

Threads of Serenity

In a cozy nook, I nestle down,
The world fades out, I wear my crown.
Pillow soft like a cloud's embrace,
In dreamland's dance, I find my pace.

Snores are symphonies, oh so grand,
I rule the kingdom of slumberland.
A nap's my quest, the dreamer's flight,
For every doze, a royal night.

Where Dreams Begin

A gentle yawn, a stretch so wide,
I find my peace, I take a ride.
Beneath the sheets, a world unknown,
Adventures bloom in dreams alone.

With cheeky cats and popcorn skies,
I chase the stars where laughter lies.
Each snoozy hour, a treasure chest,
In naptime's realm, I'm truly blessed.

A Garden of Tranquil Thoughts

In fields of pillows, dreams take root,
With fluffy clouds, my favorite loot.
A nap is planting seeds of cheer,
Awake, I'll bloom, with no more fear.

Sunbeams tickle, I squint and grin,
As zany thoughts begin to spin.
Doodles of snooze in colors bright,
In each short rest, I find delight.

Napping in the Bliss of Existence

The clock ticks slow in blissful trance,
Just one more snooze—oh, what a chance!
Worldly worries, they slip away,
In dream's embrace, I love to play.

Slippers on, I glide with ease,
In sleepy realms, I do as I please.
Each nap a gift, a playful tease,
In life's great game, I take my freeze.

Serenity's Secret

In the glow of afternoon light,
A pillow beckons, oh what delight!
With soft whispers, it calls my name,
To the land where dreams play a game.

The world outside may still spin and twirl,
But here in my slumber, I'm king of the world!
Chasing clouds on a fluffy jet stream,
In this sweet escape, I can finally dream.

Nap-Time Narratives

Once upon a sofa, I found my bliss,
With a cozy blanket and a gentle kiss.
Timmy the cat joins me in repose,
In this kingdom of cushions, anything goes!

Adventures await in the deep fluffy haze,
Where I ride on unicorns through the sun's warm rays.
A snack bar in the clouds, oh what a treat!
Who knew a nap could be such a feat?

The Depths of Dreamland

In dreamland's depths, where time stands still,
I wrestle with dragons, what a thrill!
Mermaids sing lullabies soft and sweet,
While I nap like a champ, oh what a feat!

With snickers of laughter, we dance and we spin,
As the sandman chuckles at the chaos within.
Tickle fights with shadows, a whimsical scene,
Life's troubles dissolve, so serene, so keen!

Essence of a Short Escape

A dash to the couch, a leap in the air,
With dreams like candy, I float without care.
The clock's ticking softly, but I do not mind,
In this fleeting moment, pure joy I find.

A quick trip to snooze town, oh what a delight,
With giggles and chuckles, I dance through the night.
Each second is magic, each minute a gem,
Who knew that a nap could be life's perfect hymn?

The Poetry Found in Hibernation

In winter's chill, we cuddle tight,
Dreaming dreams of fuzzy delight.
With blankets piled high and far,
We snooze away beneath the stars.

The world may spin, but here we lay,
As snuggly bears, we start to sway.
Beneath the sheets, we laugh and snore,
A symphony of snores galore!

Life's big questions fade to gray,
When eyelids droop and whisk us away.
We trade our worries for a sigh,
And let the cozy hours fly by.

So here's to naps, the sweetest art,
Where dreams and giggles fill the heart.
In hibernation, let's unite,
And find our fun in nap times bright.

The Dance of Drowsiness

Oh, what a performance we begin,
With half-closed eyes, we let life spin.
A tango of yawns and sleepy grins,
In the waltz of dreams, our trip begins.

The bed, our stage, the pillows, our crew,
In slumber's embrace, there's much to do.
We pirouette into cotton clouds,
While laughter spills in slumberous crowds.

With every snooze, a new dance unfolds,
As we twirl through blankets, brave and bold.
In the rhythm of naps, our spirits rise,
A jig of joy beneath slumbering skies.

So let's rejoice in drowsy delight,
And dance like no one's watching tonight.
For in every doze, we lose the chase,
And find our hearts at a slower pace.

Rest, Reflect, Renew

When eyelids droop, it's time to pause,
To ponder life without a cause.
In gentle slumber, wisdom creeps,
Where thoughts take flight in quiet leaps.

With every breath, we drift away,
To lands where giggles come to play.
Reflection comes like a fluffy cloud,
In nap's embrace, we feel so proud.

Renewing zest with every yawn,
As sunlight spills, we greet the dawn.
In restful moments, chaos shrinks,
Where joy is found in sleepy winks.

So hush the noise, let silence bloom,
In cozy corners, there's always room.
For rest brings clarity, sweet and true,
In nap's embrace, we start anew.

The Softness of a Sweet Escape

In moments still, we float away,
To lands where sleepyhead can play.
With dreams like candy, soft and sweet,
Our worries fade as we retreat.

Oh, treasure naps like hidden gold,
Where tales of rest are often told.
In fluffy clouds, we spin and roll,
As giggles bubble from the soul.

The world outside may rush and race,
But in this comfort, we find our pace.
A soft escape from daily strife,
Lost in the warmth of napping life.

So let's indulge in this delight,
As pillow forts become our flight.
In the softness of slumber's arms,
We find our peace, with all its charms.

The Slumbering Soul's Inquiry

When eyelids droop, the world fades
Questions float like cotton candy
Is it wisdom or just snooze time?
In dreams, who needs a plan?

Counting sheep in silly socks,
A quest for z's, oh what a trip!
Sleepy thoughts, a giggling flock,
Nap time's the ultimate script.

Snores are life's sweet symphony,
Tangled in sheets, a cozy finale,
Awake with crumbs of yesterday's snack,
Life's answers might be on this track.

So rest your head, oh curious mind,
For every dream hides a few laughs.
When we rise, we shall find,
A truth tucked in our napping halves.

Dreams in a Pillowed Universe

A pillow soft like marshmallow fluff,
An adventure begins in cozy land,
Racing sheep and flying ducks,
Who knew napping's so well planned?

Chasing dreams on a fluffy cloud,
Giggles echo in the night,
Is it magic or just me, loud?
The sandman brings the best delight.

Naps are portals, no need for keys,
Off to worlds that flip and sway,
In pajamas we fight time like bees,
Snooze awards for best display!

Awake or asleep, the prize is clear,
A funny riddle, wisdom's jest,
Find a cozy chair, dear, my dear,
For life's answers come with a rest.

The Restful Riddle

Nap or think? A pickle awaits,
Life's a puzzle, wrapped in sheets,
Toss and turn, what awaits?
A snooze-capped mind just can't be beat.

Coffee brews with dreams on the side,
Clocks don't matter in this game,
On a cloud, I'll take my ride,
What's their secret? Who's to blame?

With blankets like capes, I take flight,
A champion snoozer, hear my cheer!
All the answers come in twilight,
When my mind slips into the weird.

So laugh it off, embrace the fluff,
Life's meaning is tucked in a yawn,
For every nap, the riddle's tough,
Find peace in dreams, till the dawn.

Whispered Wisdom of Sleep

In the realm of cozy dreams,
Wisdom whispers through the night,
On pillows soft, the laughter beams,
Napping truths come into sight.

Snooze away the day-to-day,
Nonsense dances in your head,
With every snooze, come what may,
The world can wait, or it's misled.

Slumber parties with sleepy bunnies,
Pajama-clad, we plot and scheme,
Life's riddles are filled with funnies,
Reality's just a funny dream.

So tip your hat to yawning hours,
And chuckle at the z's you reap,
For wisdom blooms like blooming flowers,
In the whispered winds of sleep.

The Craft of Closing Eyes

In a chair by the sun, I take my seat,
Drifting in the world of dreams so sweet.
Thoughts float like clouds, just passing by,
Reality fades, I let out a sigh.

The clock tick-tocks, but I don't care,
Caught in a moment, floating in air.
No emails, no meetings, just a soft snore,
The joy of snoozing, oh, who could want more?

Pillows like clouds, each crevice I find,
In the kingdom of nap, I'm truly unconfined.
A yawn, a stretch, then back to the bliss,
In a world full of chaos, this is pure bliss.

So here's to the dreamers, both near and far,
Masters of napping, shining like a star.
With every closed eye, life's troubles can fade,
In the art of napping, true wisdom cascades.

Naptime Epiphanies

Lying down, I ponder deep and wide,
What's the meaning? I can't decide.
Maybe it's snacks or a cozy retreat,
Or just a good nap with a pillow so sweet.

Waking to thunder, but it's just my snores,
Golden ideas behind closed doors.
A philosophy formed in dreams so grand,
Transforms into wisdom, just like I planned.

The couch is my throne; the blanket my cape,
In this napping realm, I gallantly escape.
Each moment of slumber, a treasure I seek,
As I slink into dreams, oh, do not disturb this peak!

Awake now, I ponder my zany adventures,
Fluffy clouds merging, bright sunlit censures.
Napping reveals truths we never could grasp,
In 40 winks, I let the world unclasp.

Unraveling Life's Daydreams

Life's a circus, juggling at best,
But rest is the key to the ultimate quest.
In the arms of Morpheus, all logic is bliss,
I nap like a champ; it's my favorite kiss.

Awake, I realize I forgot all my woes,
While dreaming of travels and flamboyant clothes.
Each slumbering sigh is like a magic spell,
Twisting my worries into stories to tell.

Mornings are tricky, but naps are pure gold,
In the realm of dreams, I'm brave and I'm bold.
So I close my eyes, adventure awaits,
Each nap is a journey through whimsical gates.

When the snooze button beckons, I give in with glee,
Life's quirks dissolve as I drift towards the sea.
Floating through moments, unwrapped, grand and free,
I find all the answers, as I cuddle with me.

Chronicles of Breathtaking Naps

Once upon a time, in a land of repose,
Stood a kingdom where slumber freely flows.
Bravely the dreamers gathered their might,
To plunge into napland, from morning till night.

With blankets as capes and pillows like steeds,
They conquered life's chaos with napping as creed.
In meetings, in traffic, they closed their sweet eyes,
Catching dreams under a blanket of skies.

The clock strikes, but who truly cares?
When adventure calls from those cushy lairs.
Each yawn is a call to the throne of the rest,
In the chronicles of naps, we are truly blessed.

So gather, dear dreamers, together we lie,
In the realms of our slumber, our spirits can fly.
Through laughter and dreams, our tales intertwine,
In the art of napping, we surely shine!

Rest as Resistance

When the world is loud, I take my stance,
A cozy blanket, a sleepy trance.
Protest through dreams, let worries slide,
In the land of snooze, I'm filled with pride.

Ticking clocks, they just can't win,
I'll nap again, let the games begin.
Behind closed eyes, rebellion brews,
For every fluff, I'll gladly snooze.

Leisure's laughter, my battle cry,
Subdued by pillows, I aim for the sky.
Resistance strong in every yawn,
As dreams parade, my cares are gone.

So here's to slumber, the greatest plight,
In pillows deep, I find my light.
With every nap, I write my tale,
In restful pages, I shall prevail.

Hibernation of the Heart

When winter calls and days grow cold,
I seek the warmth, oh, dreams unfold.
A cozy cave, my heart's retreat,
In this soft space, I feel complete.

With eyelids heavy, I nestle deep,
Where cuddly critters like to sleep.
In fuzzy thoughts, love's warmth ignites,
Hibernation wraps, as joy invites.

While others rush, my spirit soars,
In fluffy pillows, I hear the roars.
Of creatures snoring in perfect tune,
As I drift to sleep beneath the moon.

So guard your heart, and slip away,
In cozy sighs, we find our play.
For in sweet dreams, we softly dwell,
A hibernation where all is well.

The Dreamer's Inquiry

What's the answer, oh gentle night?
Do dreams reveal the soul's delight?
With every snore, I ask the stars,
In my quest for truth, should I raise bars?

Hand to pillow, questions abound,
Do answers hide in sleep profound?
As I float on clouds of fluffy white,
Are they the keys to inner light?

Beyond the slumber, I seek a clue,
In realms of twilight, I barter too.
But waking life has chores and woes,
Still, in this cosmos, the dreamer knows.

The laughter echoes through night's embrace,
Each silly thought becomes a chase.
So here I lie, with sleep's sweet kiss,
In dreams I ponder, the world's pure bliss.

Reverie's Soft Touch

A gentle sigh sweeps across my face,
In reverie's hold, I find my place.
Soft whispers tease, inviting me in,
To float on clouds, let the fun begin.

Chasing shadows in the midday sun,
Does my nap mean that I've already won?
With cozy corners and soft, warm sheets,
Life's little treasures feel so sweet.

Mirthful musings dance through the haze,
In a land where dreams are fun-filled plays.
Past worries drift like feathers lost,
In reverie's touch, I find the cost.

So raise a glass to naps divine,
To cotton-candy thoughts that intertwine.
In this funny state, I drift away,
Finding joy in every playful sway.

Awakening within the Sleep

In the realm of dreams I soar,
Chasing sheep, oh, nevermore!
Snores resemble a wild tune,
As daylight breaks, I rise too soon.

Pillows whisper secrets sweet,
While blankets wrap my tired feet.
They say my snooze is quite a gift,
In slumber's clutch, my spirits lift.

Awake I sit with coffee near,
Dazed smiles reflect the night's cheer.
With blissful yawns and heavy eyes,
I ponder if sleep's the greatest prize.

Who knew a nap could spark such glee,
With dreams as fine as fine can be?
In sleepy thoughts, we laugh and play,
As naptime beckons, come what may.

The Philosophy of Tired Minds

With heavy lids, we seek the deep,
In pillows soft, our thoughts do creep.
Einstein snoozed to find the light,
Like me today, I'll nap outright.

A cat knows well the sunny spot,
In gentle dreams, we find our plot.
A nap or two may solve the test,
Just don't forget to wake and jest!

Tired brains have much to say,
In sleepy rants and creative sway.
Between each doze, great thoughts emerge,
Who knew a snooze could lead to surge?

So let's embrace our gentle plight,
In daily dozing, we find delight.
As philosophical naps expand,
We laugh at life, a funny brand.

Bedtime Musings on Tomorrow

As night descends and dreams take flight,
I ponder all that feels so right.
Tomorrow's tasks, they dance and swirl,
But now, let's nap and let it unfurl.

Tossing pillows, maybe one more spin,
In this soft haven, I'll surely win.
What's on the menu? Snacks galore!
Perhaps I dream of the kitchen floor.

Counting snacks instead of sheep,
In dreams so sweet, I'll take a leap.
With giggles echoing through the night,
I wriggle in slumber; it just feels right.

So here's to naps—a funny plight,
In slumber's grasp, we embrace the light.
Awake or asleep? It's quite a game,
Tomorrow will wait, it's never the same.

Fleeting Moments of Existence

In fleeting dreams, we chase a laugh,
With silly thoughts, we wander half.
Moments blur like coffee's steam,
Awake and napping—a glorious theme.

The clock ticks slowly, or so it seems,
As I float in and out of dreams.
A wink, a nod, they stay awhile,
Then off they go to make me smile.

Through napping hours, life seems grand,
With wrinkled sheets, I take a stand.
Philosophers nod at time's cruel jest,
While I just nap, it's truly the best.

Embrace the fun of sleepy lines,
Where silly dreams draw joyful signs.
In naps we find life's sweetest pact,
So close your eyes and don't look back.

Meditations of the Mind's Eye

In the stillness, dreams take flight,
Cushions soft as clouds in sight.
Thoughts drift like feathers on a breeze,
Napping with purpose, oh, what ease!

A snooze so sweet, it feels divine,
Time bends, and stars align.
Snoring softly, I conquer worlds,
In cozy realms where joy unfurls.

Life's great quest is simply this,
A comfy spot, a gentle bliss.
When all is quiet, wisdom speaks,
As eyelids droop and sunlight peeks.

Awake with giggles, what a delight,
Life's meaning found in dreams at night.
With one last yawn and a stretch so grand,
I drift off again—oh, isn't it planned!

The Weight of a Feather

A pillow's embrace, oh so light,
I slip into slumber, what a sight!
With dreams that tickle, thoughts that play,
I lounge like royalty, come what may.

The weight of a feather, I float on air,
Chasing sandman tales without a care.
Oh, what mischief in pillow fights,
As giggles echo through endless nights.

Coffee's for the brave, naps are for the wise,
In a fortress of blankets—my grand prize.
Close my eyes, the world turns gray,
In feather-filled realms, I giggle away.

When the day resumes, I stretch and sigh,
"Why run the race?" I ask with a smile.
For wisdom found in snoozy charms,
Rests in the comfort of warm surrounds.

In the Arms of Quietude

Whispers of silence pull me near,
In cozy corners, free from fear.
As eyelids flutter, dreams begin,
In the arms of quietude, I win.

Like clouds of candy, my thoughts disperse,
Wandering realms, oh, how diverse!
With every snooze, new adventures sprout,
Life's greatest riddle, isn't that about?

Silly worries float, I'm unconfined,
In naptime magic, peace I find.
Fuzzy critters dance on dreamy streams,
Under the banner of whimsical dreams.

But wake me gently, the sun is high,
Laughter spills out, oh my, oh my!
For in quiet arms, I played and spun,
Life's vibrant colors, naps just begun.

Nap Bliss

A nap, my friend, is a treasure's key,
Unlocking joys so blissfully.
With blankets wrapped like a warm embrace,
I drift to a land, a sleepy place.

When the world demands, I simply decline,
In realms of snores, everything's fine.
A giggle erupts from deep within,
Life's little secrets—no need to spin.

The world rushes by, but I am still,
In my fluff fortress, dreams fulfill.
Tick-tock, tick-tock, the clock slyly pranks,
While I'm riding moonbeams and sailing the banks.

So, when you ponder life's complex scheme,
Remember the magic of a good dream.
For in those soft pauses, laughter finds,
The joy of existence that naps unwinds!

Reflections in a Dream

Who needs philosophers with cozy beds?
A pillow's embrace, where thought treads.
Eyes softly close, the world fades away,
In realms of slumber, we frolic and play.

Drool on my chin, yet wisdom unfolds,
In dreams, I'm a king, with treasures untold.
Snoring symphonies, a concert so grand,
The art of napping, my preferred brand.

Life's riddles solved with a snooze and a grin,
In the tapestry of dreams, I find my win.
Beneath the soft sheets, revelations take flight,
What's profound by day is hilarious by night.

So laugh at the critics, let the debate rage,
For in peaceful slumber, I write my own page.
A lighthearted life, where naps are the key,
To both joy and wisdom, I rest, and I'm free.

Tides of Rest

The clock strikes noon, my eyelids collide,
With comfy cushions, my stress, I confide.
In the ocean of dreams, I drift on a sea,
Riding waves of slumber, wild, fast, and free.

With each little nap, I gather my thoughts,
In this cozy harbor, anxiety rots.
The tides pull me under, but I don't resist,
For humor and rest make the perfect twist.

When I wake with a grin, pearls of wisdom abound,
Just remind me of chores when my head hits the ground.
A sailor of slumber, navigating delight,
Beneath the soft blanket, I dance through the night.

So here's to the snoozers, the dreamers, the bold,
In the tide of repose, our laughter is gold.
Life's not just work—oh, what a jest!
It's napping on couches, now that's the best!

Serenity in Stillness

In silence, I ponder, no tick-tock in sight,
The allure of stillness, oh what a delight.
A blanket cocoon, I slip deep inside,
With dreams as my compass, I take off and glide.

Life's all a race, like a hamster in spin,
But I find my peace in the snores from within.
Oh, the joy of pausing, a whimsical pause,
In the comfort of dreams, I throw out the laws.

The world's a stage, yet I've lost my cue,
In the theater of naptime, I know what to do.
With chuckles and yawns intertwined in my mind,
I bask in their warmth, as I dawdle and unwind.

So raise up a toast to the quietest plea—
A nap is a treasure that's truly for me.
In stillness, I find what's humorous and bright,
For life is much funnier when napping feels right.

The Art of Pausing

With coffee in hand and work in a haze,
I ponder the beauty of naptime displays.
A snooze here, a wiggle, a chuckle or two,
Tick-tock goes the clock, but what do I do?

I pause like a painter, brush strokes of sleep,
Creating a canvas so vivid and deep.
With snuggly soft blankets and pillows galore,
I enter the gallery of dreams to explore.

Life's puzzle dissolves as I sink in my dreams,
With fluffy pink clouds and chocolate streams.
As giggles of joy fill my slumbering state,
I chuckle at worries, I just can't relate.

So let's perfect this art, let's make it a trend,
To laugh while we snooze, to pause and transcend.
In the gallery of napping, oh what a delight,
For life's funny moments shine brightest at night.

The Restful Riddle

When life gets rough, just take a break,
Snooze a bit, for goodness' sake.
Dreams may slip like toes in sand,
A nap's the cure to understand.

Tick-tock goes the weary clock,
But on my pillow, I'm a rock.
Questions fade in cozy bliss,
If snoozing's wrong, then what is this?

With snuggled sheets and heavy eyes,
I find deep truths 'neath slumber's skies.
Waking up, the world's a joke,
Maybe wisdom's just a yoke!

So blame life's woes on daytime haste,
Sometimes a snooze is what you taste.
For when you snuggle down with zeal,
You tap the truth—a nap is real!

Pillows and Philosophy

With soft pillows, thoughts disperse,
Each nap a point in life's far verse.
Philosophers would likely agree,
Nap time's a key to finding glee.

Epicurus would raise a toast,
To sleepyheads who love the most.
In cozy realms where dreams reside,
We ponder all, yet still abide.

The world spins madly, what a mess,
But on my bed, I find success.
I'll challenge Kant—did he ever yawn?
These sleepy dreams, we'll carry on!

So let the day keep marching by,
In fluffy clouds, I'll snooze and sigh.
Life's puzzles fade in the night's embrace,
A nap, it seems, has its own grace.

Between Awakenings

Awake, then snooze, a loop I make,
Each time I drift, the more I quake.
What's life about? I shall decide,
With blinks and naps, let truth abide.

Between the snoozes, life unfolds,
With jokes and jests, the world retold.
Napping wisdom drips like rain,
As dreams float soft beneath my brain.

The ultimate quest is tucked in tight,
In blankets warm, I find delight.
So when the questions start to creep,
I shut my eyes and fall to sleep.

And if you ask me, "What's the score?"
I'll yawn and say, "Just one more snore!"
For in a dream, we find what's grand,
In whispered fluff and slumber's hand.

The Poetry of Pause

In the hustle where the busy race,
Pillow kingdoms hold a tranquil space.
Each quiet sigh and peaceful breath,
A rhythmic dance that masters death.

In naps, I find my fleeting muse,
Where thoughts can giggle and ideas fuse.
The world spins on, but here I'm still,
In dreamy depths, I find my thrill.

Philosophy? It's all quite fuzzy,
Between the snores, the mind gets dizzy.
Awkward truths, like sheets, unwind,
In slumber's grip, what gems we find!

So wade through naps without a care,
For in those moments, life lays bare.
With laughter stitched in cozy seams,
Napping's the poetry of dreams.

The Art of Lethargic Reflection

In the depths of a couch so divine,
Where the cushions embrace, that space is mine.
Dreamland tango with a whispering sigh,
Who needs the world when the eyelids comply?

My thoughts flutter off like wayward cats,
Chasing dust motes in sunbeams like bats.
Naps are a canvas for dreams to collage,
Life's great mysteries—oh, how they dislodge!

A sandwich half-eaten sits cold on my plate,
While my mind wanders off—poverty of fate.
Do I ponder existence, or just the snacks?
Surely the answer's down here in the racks!

So here I recline with a satisfied grin,
In the embrace of my blanket, let's not begin.
Philosophers ponder while I take a leap,
Here's the wisdom of napping, in slumber, I reap.

Pillowtalk with Existence

Oh pillow, confessor of my dreams untold,
What secrets you keep, all warm and bold.
Life's queries dissolve in your soft embrace,
How profound it is, this sleepy space.

Do you think of the cosmos as I drift away?
Or just count the sheep who in slumber play?
My eyelids close slowly, like curtains of night,
Under the starlit blankie, all feels just right.

Awake, I ponder—what has life's cost?
Yet on this cushion, I feel like a boss.
With each gentle snore, a philosopher grows,
In a nap, the universe seems to propose.

Is an hour of dozing worth more than a lecture?
That fine line of thinking, oh what a texture!
So let's toast to the dreams, and let thoughts be free,
In pillowtalk with existence, it's just you and me.

The Gentle Philosophy of Napping

In the classroom of bed, I earn my degree,
With credits in snoozing and mastery.
A lecture on fluff, a seminar's tease,
Philosophy teaches, 'Just rest if you please.'

Under the blue sky of eyelids so tight,
I'll ponder the questions in the soft twilight.
What is bliss, but a moment of rest?
Asking profound things is frankly a jest.

Awake, or asleep? Who calls it a crime?
In the land of the nappers, we've found perfect time.
The greats may have wisdom, but look at my flair—
A few lazy moments can rival a stare.

So when asked about meaning, just flash a warm smile,
The gentle philosophy stretches a while.
With a pillow as teacher, let worries just roam,
In the world of thoughts napping, I feel right at home.

Siestas and Significance

To nap or not to nap, that's the grandest question,
With schedules so tight, I crave some discretion.
The sun's lazy rays beckon me near,
What's meant to be pondered can wait till next year.

A cat takes its rest, wise beyond its years,
While I wrestle with thoughts, battling my fears.
But deep in the cushions, oh what sweet glee,
The secrets of life escape effortlessly.

With dreams as my guide, I float on soft clouds,
Who needs a hard chair or judgment from crowds?
In the pursuit of significance, let's reclaim truth,
For napping is wisdom, and naps are my proof.

So here's to the siestas, the soft, gentle art,
Where meaning is found, making hearts serenely start.
In the grand design of a well-napped day,
Every snooze is a lesson, come what may.

A Hug from the Universe

In the cozy realm of pillow dreams,
Clouds whisper secrets, or so it seems.
Tickle your thoughts, let worries drift,
Naptime's the universe's perfect gift.

Snore like a bear in the afternoon sun,
Life's heavy questions, on hold, just for fun.
Basking in comfort, in soft, feathery light,
A snooze is the answer, it feels just right.

Jokes of existence float soft in the air,
Laughter and snoozes make for a fair share.
Why chase a meaning when pillows abound?
In fluff we find wisdom, sleepy and sound.

Floating in Quiet Waters

Drift like a leaf on a lazy lake,
Naps are the sails, let the day take its break.
Ripples of joy in the mid-afternoon,
The world can wait; please, just let me swoon.

Caffeine can wait, let's take this slow,
In a soft, little bubble, with nowhere to go.
Splashing in stillness, no worries to tend,
Caught in a current where time's just a friend.

Dreams wriggle like fish, they swim and they tease,
Why fret about problems? Just nap if you please.
Pour another cup? Not if I can nap!
In silence we linger, in pleasure we wrap.

The Essence of Being Still

Nestled in comfort, let tension unwind,
Serenity brews in the stillness we find.
Close your two peepers; let reality pause,
In the arms of a nap, we dissolve all our flaws.

Eyelids like curtains, they gently descend,
Sleepy-time's wisdom is hard to contend.
Who needs great purpose when drowsiness sings?
The essence of stillness reveals little things.

Maybe life's answers are buried in sheets,
Wrapped in the tangle of dreams so sweet.
So curl up tight, let your brain take a breather,
In stillness we ponder, wrapped in a slumber.

Forget about puzzles and riddles of fate,
An invitation to dream is a tempting mate.
Each snore is a giggle from galaxies far,
As comets collide, and naps take us far.

Moments in a Dreamscape

Slip into dreams where the grass is all fuzz,
Time slows to a crawl; what a marvelous buzz!
Lollygag, doze off, let the mind take a roam,
In the land of the snooze, everyone feels at home.

Crashes of laughter, the tickle of beams,
In bright, chirpy colors, we weave our own themes.
The realms of the silly dance in our minds,
Where questions are muffled and joy is what finds.

Plunge into pillows, take twilight's warm hand,
Hold on to the giggles, let the slumbers expand.
Unravel the chaos with a grin and a yawn,
In dreams, we are kings, and worries are gone.

Beneath the Cloud of Sleep

Beneath the cloud of drowsy dreams,
I float on pillows, or so it seems.
A world of z's, oh what a delight,
In my cozy kingdom, sleep takes flight.

Chasing sheep in a sunny field,
With every snore, my worries yield.
Tickle my toes, the day can wait,
For in this realm, I'm truly great.

The clock may tick, but I won't care,
For here in slumber, there's magic in air.
A nap is a treasure, so soft and sweet,
In dreamland, oh how we retreat.

So let the world be wild and loud,
I'll sip my dreams beneath the cloud.
With every blink of my sleepy eyes,
I find my wisdom in pillow skies.

A Symphony of Shadows

A symphony plays in the afternoon sun,
With snores as notes, we'll have some fun.
A symphony of shadows creeps,
As cozy corners call for blissful sleeps.

The couch becomes my concert hall,
While daily chatter fades to a crawl.
In dreams, I'm a maestro, leading the way,
With every soft snore, I steal the day.

My fuzzy slippers dance to the beat,
While fluffy pillows cushion each seat.
Life's chaos pauses, all strife on mute,
In this darkened symphony, I take root.

And when I awake, with a lingering grin,
I'll orchestrate joy, where napping begins.
For in this music, I find my tune,
With sleepy serenades and great afternoon.

Slumber's Gentle Hour

In slumber's gentle hour, I find my bliss,
As pillows cuddle me with a warm kiss.
A quick escape from troubles and gripes,
Where all evolving feels like a great type.

A nap is like magic, with a tiny wand,
With every doze, I travel beyond.
In odd places on a dream-filled train,
Where boredom dissolves and laughs remain.

The enemies of sleep may try to sneak,
But I'm sealed tight with a drowsy peak.
As I drift in silence, my worries drop,
In this soft world, there's no need to stop.

So let them rattle, let the world spin,
I'll harness the joy from this fleeting win.
For when I awaken, with a satisfied sigh,
I conquer the day like a nap-filled high.

Nightfall and Nostalgia

As nightfall blankets the weary town,
I sink into cushions, my heavy crown.
Nostalgia whispers in the warm gloom,
While sleep's gentle fingers chase away doom.

With visions of cookies and warm milk flows,
In this cozy realm, anything goes.
I dance with shadows as dreams unfold,
In a sleepy embrace, my heart feels bold.

The world fades away, blurring fast,
In the softness of night, I wish it could last.
With chuckles and giggles, I twirl in delight,
As sleep sweeps me up, on a blanket of night.

And when morning breaks with a bright hello,
Those funny little moments still steal the show.
Forever in slumber, I'll hold onto glee,
For in laughter of napping, we're truly free.

Whispers of the Pillow

In dreams I dance, I flip and twirl,
The pillow giggles, gives a whirl.
Do thoughts unravel in daytime's grind?
Or do they snooze, just so unkind?

A nap is wisdom, like sage on toast,
In snoozy realms, I'm the proud host.
Life's a puzzle, sleep's the clue,
So wise folks nap, it's true, it's true!

I chase the world, then hit the snooze,
Strip off the stress, I'm free to choose.
In cozy dreams, I save the day,
With pillows stacked, I rule the fray!

Close your eyes, let worries flee,
A quick embrace with tranquility.
For napping grants a joyful spree,
Who knew sleep's depth held irony?

Where Time Sleeps

Tick-tock the clock, it doesn't matter,
When eyelids drop, the world grows fatter.
Pillows promise a magic ride,
Where bedtime tales and dreams collide.

In blanket forts of fluffy dreams,
Reality fades, or so it seems.
The universe whispers, 'snooze a while,'
In dreamland, I'm a sleepystyle!

A nap is better than an hour long chat,
With nodding heads and chatter flat.
Just drift away, float on a cloud,
And snore a symphony, oh so loud!

So when life seems a dizzy race,
Try closing your eyes, find your space.
In the kingdom of snooze, we're all queen and king,
Where laughter and napping are our favorite things!

Echoes of Morning Light

The sun peeks in, I shuffle and squint,
But the bed is a fortress, and I'm the prince.
Loud alarms sing a siren song,
Yet here I lie, where dreams belong.

With sleepy grins and lazy sighs,
I cuddle my dreams, say sweet goodbyes.
Chasing laughter through the sheets,
In my cozy realm, it's fun that greets!

The coffee brews, it brews and brews,
But give me a nap, that's my kinda muse.
For wisdom sprouts from dreams divine,
Life's greatest tales are down the line.

A nap, dear friend, is more than rest,
It's a wild quest to be our best.
So let the morning light be bright,
While I savor snooze till the stars ignite!

The Language of Rest

In the kingdom of rest, I hold the key,
To unlock dreams, wild and free.
With each gentle snooze, I start to grin,
For the best adventures lie within!

While others rush, I pause with glee,
My pillow's a pal, it comforts me.
Naps translate silence into song,
In the stillness, I dance along!

So, let the world spin, let time unfold,
In cozy wraps of dreams untold.
For napping's a language, let's all partake,
Where hearts find rhythm, and worries break!

So when you ponder life's wacky jest,
Trust the power of a good ol' rest.
In every yawn lies humor and grace,
A sweet reminder to find our place!

Reverie Beneath the Stars

Beneath the stars, I find my quest,
The moon's my pillow, I must confess.
Dreaming of snacks and cozy sheets,
In slumbering silence, my joy repeats.

My thoughts take flight, like birds in the sky,
While all my worries quietly fly.
Floating on clouds, with laughter I drift,
In this soft blanket, I feel the gift.

Pillow fights with giggles, no cares to borrow,
Snoring like a bear, no hint of sorrow.
The true happiness lies not in the grind,
But in waking up, if I don't lose my mind.

So here's to the dreams where I can roam free,
Chasing my fantasies, just me and my Zs.
In this cosmic joke, I find sweet delight,
As I trade my worries for jigsawed night.

The Quiet Embrace of Night

When the sun fades, it's time for fun,
In the quiet embrace, the games have begun.
Blankets like arms, they hold me so tight,
Whispering secrets as I drift into night.

Fluffed-up pillows are my trusty crew,
In their soft company, I find what's true.
A dream about tacos, oh what a treat,
When I wake up, it's just hard to beat.

The world goes silent, my mind takes a flight,
Dancing with shadows, outsmarting the light.
With giggles and chuckles, I snooze through the hours,
Waking up later, life's quirks turn to flowers.

So let the night blanket me like a cocoon,
While dreams whip up laughter like a whimsical tune.
In dreams, I am king, a royal affair,
As the universe chuckles, and flips back my hair.

In Search of Restful Truths

Searching for wisdom in feathers and foam,
As I nestle down cozy, I find my home.
With each yawn, the world's troubles unwind,
In this sleepy realm, true peace I find.

My mind runs amok on imaginary quests,
Chasing sweet nap-time with laughter-filled jest.
The truths of the world come wrapped in a snore,
In dreams, I become what I've never been before.

Cuddled in comfort, I shout from my dream,
"Who needs enlightenment? This slumber's supreme!"
The soft sparkles of night peek in through the blinds,
As I chase silent revelations that the nap-time unwinds.

So let's toast to rest, where the nonsense spins,
The profound and ridiculous both wear big grins.
In cozy embraces, we're all on the run,
For heartfelt wisdom comes hidden—just done.

When Dreams Foster Meaning

As day turns to night, I lay down my head,
With flickering thoughts like a firefly spread.
In the quiet of darkness, my worries take flight,
Where dreams banter gently, and laughter feels right.

Oh, the joyful conundrum of zzzs and delight,
In whimsical lands that bloom in the night.
A pizza parade or a sock puppet show,
With each nod, I dance, and my happiness grows.

The questions of living? They fade into stars,
Replaced by wild beasts in colorful cars.
I slumber through puzzles that life likes to weave,
Finding clarity cloaked in sleep's sweet reprieve.

So here's to the dreams that foster our glee,
Where meaning takes naps, just like you and me.
As dawn peeks through curtains, soft and round,
I wake up, smirking at the magic I've found.

Reawakening the Soul

In the middle of the day, I lie down,
Pillow beneath my head, I wear a frown.
Dreams drift in like clouds on a sunny sky,
Time takes a break as I start to fly.

Fleeting thoughts of dishes piled high,
But a soft snore escapes, and they're left to cry.
The world can wait, I've got land to explore,
In a realm where chores can knock at the door.

Maps and charts can't plot this delight,
Adventures unfold in the stillness of night.
Worry unravels, and laughter ignites,
In the warm embrace of delightful sights.

Awake once more, I rub my eyes wide,
Did I conquer mountains or take a joyride?
With snacks in my dreams, oh, what a feat,
Life's grand mysteries taste better in sleep.

The Journey within the Nap

A cozy blanket wraps me like a hug,
The snooze button calls, I feel the tug.
In the dreamland, I'm a superhero,
Saving the world from a villain named 'Cereal'.

Floating on clouds made of giant pies,
Flying high, where gravity lies.
I dodge the workweek, and milk spills galore,
Belly-laughing hard, can't take it anymore.

Tick-tock of time, who needs such a thing?
In my slumber kingdom, I'm the queen, the king.
Caffeine's for mortals, not for my reign,
Where the sun is a cuddle, and smiles remain.

Awakening slowly, a grin on my face,
What treasures I've found in this napping space.
Dishes unwashed, yet I'm full of cheer,
For a nap is the journey I've come to revere.

The Interlude of Abundant Rest

In cozy beds where dreams collide,
The world's big worries get pushed aside.
With pillows soft, we find our place,
In snooze-town's warm, embracing grace.

A cat's purr echoes, soft and low,
While life's demands come and go.
In slumber's grip, we find our muse,
To snooze away, with nothing to lose.

Life's Lessons in Hibernation

The bears, they know a secret art,
Hibernate and take it smart.
We sweat the small stuff day by day,
But miss the naps in life's ballet.

With chocolate dreams and snacks so fine,
A pillow fort, the world's divine!
When eyelids droop, wisdom comes through,
The best advice? Just snooze a few!

Lounging with Dilemmas

I ponder deeply 'neath my sheets,
Should I rise or claim my treats?
Life's questions swirl like sheets askew,
But all I want is more time to snooze.

The fridge calls, yet I hesitate,
Deep thoughts can wait, procrastinate!
Life's puzzles, oh what a fuss,
I'll solve them all—right after us!

Revelations in the Realm of Rest

Awake or dream, which is the prize?
In sleep, who knows what wisdom lies?
With blankets snug and worlds to roam,
The best adventures await at home.

A cheeky snooze, a snore or two,
Revelations come, like morning dew.
In cozy realms where sloths prevail,
The secret's out: we nap without fail!

The Gentle Art of Rejuvenation

In the land of snores and dreams,
Where pillows are soft and time redeems.
The clock ticks slow, while eyelids droop,
A sanctuary found in the napping loop.

With cozy blankets as my throne,
I drift to worlds where I'm alone.
No chores to chase, no tasks in sight,
Just me and the clouds in soft sunlight.

A gentle snore escapes my lips,
While reality does silent slips.
In this fleeting pause, joy climbs high,
As laughter echoes - 'just one more try!'

So here's to naps, oh what a thrill,
The perfect potion for a sweeter chill.
We rise again, like vibrant springs,
Rejuvenated, ready for what life brings!

Sleep's Silent Symphony

In the hush of eve, with a wink and a yawn,
I close my eyes as the day moves on.
The blanket wraps like a warm embrace,
In dreams, I dance without leaving a trace.

A concert of snores fills the air anew,
As sleepyheads gather under skies so blue.
The rhythm of rest is a delightful tune,
Conducted by dreams, beneath the moon.

With each gentle sigh, worries fade away,
Muffin-top monsters holding sway.
In this lighthearted world where snooze reigns supreme,
Nap time's a treasure, a soft little dream.

Awake from my slumber with a not-so-fresh face,
But oh! Those five minutes, what a blissful space.
In Sleep's quiet symphony, all life's troubles cease,
Embrace those moments, let chaos release!

Shadows of Short Rest

In corners of couches, I seek my retreat,
Where sunlight creeps and relaxation's sweet.
A quick little doze, in the midst of the fuss,
As cat naps remind me, there's no need to rush.

The world continues, while I take a break,
With dreams that take flight, for my sanity's sake.
In shadows of short rests, I find my delight,
As the clock laughs softly, 'Just one more night!'

Oh, the giggles of naps, those sneaky little traps,
That catch weary minds in their cozy laps.
With whimsical visions, I slip under ease,
And wake up anew with a silly sneeze.

So here's to the moments that make snooze such art,
Those shadows of rest play a humorous part.
For life and its meaning, I'll take napping cheer,
In rhythmic surrender, I find joy sincere!

Brief Retreats

In a world that buzzes, I find my delight,
A brief retreat calls, it's a cozy invite.
With a swoosh of the blanket, I nestle quite low,
And surrender sweet time, letting worries all go.

Oh, the joy of the snooze, it's just so divine,
Where dreams twinkle brightly like stars that align.
For in fleeting moments, we take a quick ride,
To magical lands where our giggles collide.

When the clock seems to grumble and pull at my skin,
I chuckle and nudge it, 'Please don't let me in!'
For in naps, I meet sides of me soft and bright,
Where sleep's little secrets laugh through the night.

So welcome the pauses, those winks of delight,
In brief little retreats, may your soul take flight.
Here's to quick naps, a funny little treat,
For in a sleepy life, there's nothing quite sweet!